(Mid-Eighteenth Century)

SHIRLEY
CHARLES CITY COUNTY, VA.

COLONIAL INTERIORS

THE COLONIAL AND EARLY FEDERAL PERIODS

FIRST SERIES

by

LEIGH FRENCH JR. ~ A.I.A.

WITH AN INTRODUCTION BY
CHARLES OVER CORNELIUS

BONANZA BOOKS · NEW YORK

FOREWORD

URING the last decade, in the mad rush for architectural rejuvenation, few have had the time and opportunity to make a very careful survey of the interior architecture of our early domestic work.

The frequent publication of books on most phases of this subject has had its good effect, but they have been perhaps too reticent as to the interior arrangement and woodwork of the houses in which our forefathers lived.

In reviewing these old houses one constantly notes the analogy between them and the contemporary buildings in England. Whether the similarity in design to be observed in so many of them was the result of the constant influence on the work of the colonies by the mother country, or whether they were simply divergent through related branches of the earlier work in England, it is difficult to determine.

We know that communication with England was regular, and that there was a constant interchange of architectural ideas, both in the form of books, by personal visits, and the immigration of architects and men of all the crafts.

My idea in compiling this book is to offer to the architect and layman a more complete summary of the various existing examples of early American interiors, and I have endeavored to make it primarily a pictorial summary rather than a documentary one.

Even within a field of such obvious limitations, a work of this kind involves indebtedness to many; my thanks are here tendered to those who have most generously helped me by the loan and gift of photographs and measurements: to my friend Donald Green Tarpley, for his companionship and assistance in our trips for data; to The Society for the Preservation of New England Antiquities, for measurements of the Swett house in Newbury, Mass.; to Walter G. Davis, Esq., for the gift of photographs of the Davis house at Limington, Me.; to the Arden Studios, for photographs of the Tebbs house at Dumfries; to The Brooklyn Museum, for photographs of the Henry Sewall house at Secretary, Md.; to Harold Donaldson Eberlein, Esq., for the gift of the photographs of Shirley, Harwood House, and Whitehall; to Thomas Nash, Esq., for the photographs of Glebe house; to The Winslow Associates, for photographs of Winslow house, at Marshfield, Mass.; to Topsfield Historical Society, for the Capen house; to George F. Noyes, of Newburyport, for the photographs of the Waters and Atkinson houses; to Miss Mary Harrod Northend, for photographs of the following houses: John Whipple, Isaac Royall, The Lindens, Saltonstall, Craddock, Dalton Club, Adden, Jeremiah Lee, Quincy, Governor Wentworth, and the Pierce-Nichols; Kenneth Clark, for photographs of the following houses: Sewall, at York, Me., McCreery, Webb, Champion, Morris, Samuel Mather, Oldgate, Sigourney, Jessup, Huntington, Captain Lee, Rochambeau-Vernon, and the Dauntless Club; to Frank Cousins, for photographs of the following houses: Octagon, Jeremiah Lee, Kittridge, Oak Hill, Samuel Fowler, Stephen Swett, Pierce-Nichols, Short, Cook-Oliver, Bowker, Richard Derby, Lindall-Barnard, Stenton, Whitby Hall, Independence Hall, Robertson, Moses Williams, The Old Manse, George Cabot, Wayside Inn, Hancock-Clarke, Rockingham Hotel; Philip B. Wallace, for photographs of the following houses: George Read, Mount Pleasant, Whitby Hall, Tookermann, Roxborough, Wister, Third and Delancey Streets, Belmont, Independence Hall, Octagon, Hope Lodge, No. 47 South Sixth Street, No. 402 South Front Street, Graeme Park; the Essex Institute, for the John Ward House; to H. P. Cook, for photographs of Lower Brandon, Tuckahoe, and Westover.

LEIGH FRENCH, JR.
New York,
August, 1923.

INTRODUCTION

THE Colonial Architecture of the seventeenth and eighteenth centuries and the post-Colonial work of the early years of the Republic constitute an artistic possession of which our country has become somewhat tardily aware. This delightful work, so much of which possesses real distinction, serves both as a link with the past and as a guide for the future.

The tradition which it represents has been of continuous growth. From century to century and from country to country this tradition had spread, ever adding to itself new qualities of structure or decoration as it responded to the varied needs and tastes of the nations in which it thrived. It was associated most closely with the civilization of the west, although its earliest roots were laid in eastern soil. From early Greece to Renaissance England is a far cry, but the distance was traversed by such easy stages, by such natural growth, that its course is not difficult to follow.

The ideals of this architectural tradition of western Europe were those which the colonists to America brought with them when they introduced the standards of western civilization into the new continent. The study of how this tradition was acted upon by influences of climate and material, by economic and social characteristics, and by the taste and craftsmanship in the new country, comprises a fascinating chapter in the history of art.

The first permanent settlers in the colonies brought with them the traditions of sixteenth-century provincial England. In the great houses of the English nobles the influence of the Renaissance had begun to predominate; but in the modest homes of the middle class, the small manors and peasant cottages, the late Gothic flavor of sixteenth-century England had not been disturbed. The early settlers in New England were of this middle class, whose preferences were wholly in favor of those forms with which they were familiar and in whose construction their craftsmen were well versed.

For this reason, the earliest work in the new country carried on the late Gothic traditions of Elizabethan England, houses with steep gables and high pitched roofs, overhanging upper stories, small windows often leaded and with a structure whose disposition recalled the half-timber work in which the builders were skilled. The high pitched roofs were of practical use to shed the heavy snowfall of the long winters; the overhanging stories were relics of the medieval town dwelling and were transplanted without the compulsion of necessity in the new land.

The interiors of this period were simple and crude. The one or two room floor plan centered about the great chimney whose enormous fireplace dominated one wall of each room. This fireplace wall was frequently covered with wooden planks set vertically, their joints moulded. The ceiling, heavily beamed, was constructed usually with a great central summer beam into which were entered the smaller beams, carrying from it to the outside walls. The walls of the rooms might be roughly plastered, sheathed with boards the whole of their height or a part of it. The windows were small, set high and, when glass was used, fitted with leaded quarries in the casements. The floors of wide boards were covered with rush or clean sea-sand.

The furniture of the times was comparatively large in scale, and the essential quality of a room of this period was the curious one of scale given by large and heavy furniture in comparatively small and low ceiled rooms.

Toward the end of the seventeenth century and by the early years of the eighteenth century, the Italian influences, which had by that time finally established themselves in England, began to find their way to America with the increasing frequency of communication. The exterior signs of their change in taste and usage are contained in the symmetrical placing of the windows and doors, the emphasis upon horizontality rather than verticality, by the use of band courses and definitely marked cornices, and the employment of dormer windows.

On the interiors the change is noticed in the covering of the beams with a plastered ceiling, the introduction of stile and rail paneling, the tendency to increase the ceiling heights, the enlargement of the window openings, which were filled with double hung sash with wood muntins, and in some cases the reduction in size of the fireplace openings. The plan, too, had evolved into a greater elaboration. The central hall running through the house and four rooms opening from it, the stairway as an architectural feature, two or four chimneys at the ends of the house rather than one in the center, are a few of the innovations which marked this important change in taste. Such changes were not alone dictated by taste, but were equally influenced by economic conditions. Much of the old tradition in planning lingered, particularly in the frontier section, well along into the late eighteenth century, and no hard and fast rule can be laid down for the beginning of a certain innovation or the end of a particular usage.

The decorative elements of the interior chiefly distinguish these earlier eighteenth-century houses from those of the latter half of the century. The run mouldings are bold, almost coarse in scale; there is comparatively little carved decoration and that confined to a simple spotting of detail, the bolection moulding finds its place around the fireplaces and in some cases around wall panels. The simple quarter-round moulding frames most of the panels of the wainscot, while architrave details were universally applied to window enframement. Mantel shelves were the exception rather than rule, and little or no use of pilasters occurred. The woodwork and walls, if the latter were unpaneled, were painted in strong colors, the floors, too, were frequently painted, sometimes stenciled in designs.

The work of the mid-eighteenth century carried on in general the same features as those mentioned above. There was a slightly increased refinement in detail, a more architectonic use of orders and classic motives, carving was used more freely in mantelpieces, cornices and trim mingled with a more or less correct use of dentils, modillions, and other repeating forms from the classic tradition. A greater sophistication is noticeable in a careful study of plan decoration and proportion.

It is in this period that many very large houses were built, since the time was one of considerable prosperity. Communication with England was steady and increasing, and ideas of sophisticated living were taking root among the more well-to-do colonists.

This particular period in the history of the architecture carried through until the Revolution. The years of war interrupted both the influx of new ideas from abroad and the growth of wealth. When again the country, now an independent nation, began to think of building, the taste of Europe had changed and the changed influence was felt in the United States.

This work of the last part of the eighteenth and early part of the nineteenth century confesses an increased attenuation and refinement in line, proportion, and detail. It followed as closely as possible the ultra sophistication of the work of Robert Adam which its designers knew by means of published works which were current in this country.

In plan, in carefully studied elevations, in delicate detail, and in fine proportion these houses present the natural goal of the changes and development of the preceding seventy-five years.

The interiors, lofty and well proportioned, were chastely enhanced with delicate trim. The cornices and mantelpieces were often enriched by the application of composition ornament, reminiscent of the Adam Brothers, the detail of this ornament relying upon the rejuvenated forms of late Roman motives. Paneling was restricted to the walls below the chair-rail and to the overmantel and sides of the chimney-breast.

In plan, the space relation of rooms one to another and their variety in shape—circular, octagonal, and oval as well as rectangular —marked a greater self-consciousness in the academic study of design.

The governmental usage of the new country gave opportunity for more monumental forms of building than anything hitherto attempted, and the types of governmental architecture laid the foundation for the best tradition which we have for republican state and national building.

And here lies the chief importance of this old work which has again come into its own. It holds a vital message for the American architect to-day.

The nineteenth century saw the complete breakdown in the great tradition in building which had continued, up to then, unbroken. This breakdown was so complete that at the opening of the twentieth century no trace of a tradition remained. The efforts of the architects of this comparatively recent time lead, in the search of a tradition, to the trying out of every sort of architectural style of the past. Among those attempted was the so-called Colonial with results which appear to-day, so often, murderous. But the study of early American architecture continued, and many people will not hesitate to admit that the qualities inherent in the work of our forefathers are those which have a real congeniality with the conditions and life of this country. Particularly in domestic work is this true, and the successful houses built in the early American tradition certainly outnumber by far those built in any purely European style.

No slavish copying of the old work will produce sincere and living architecture, but the greatest element of instruction to be gained from the study of such interiors as are shown in this volume lies in an appreciation of how our early builders translated the forms of European work into a vernacular which they so well understood.

With a general knowledge of the origin of the forms from which these builder-architects derived their inspiration, it is not difficult to learn just where they chose to simplify or where to elaborate upon the original. Freely they juggled the elements of their form and decoration, their scale and proportion. Sometimes they erred, more often they attained a distinctive character which more knowing men could not achieve, but always they were sincere and always imbued with a high ideal.

In urging, then, a return to the old tradition which for two hundred years thrived happily in American soil, we are not interested alone in the forms in which this tradition expressed itself, but we are equally concerned with the ideals and ideas behind it, which gave it its particular flavor so well suited to the tastes and usage of Americans both now and of yore.

CHARLES OVER CORNELIUS.

LIST OF PLATES

Frontispiece—Shirley, Charles City County, Va.

INTERIORS

List of Plates

List of Plates

List of Plates

List of Plates

List of Plates

CHRONOLOGY OF THE ILLUSTRATIONS

Mid-Seventeenth Century
> Plates 1, 2, 3, 57, 58, 72.

Late Seventeenth Century
> Plates 4, 5, 6, 7, 8, 59, 72.

Early Eighteenth Century
> Plates 8, 9, 10, 11, 12, 34, 60, 61, 62, 63, 64, 65, 105.

Mid-Eighteenth Century
> Frontispiece
> Plates 13, 14, 15, 16, 17, 18, 19, 20, 21, 35, 36, 37, 38, 39,
> 58, 60, 64, 65, 66, 67, 68, 69, 70, 71, 87, 88, 89, 90,
> 91, 92, 103, 104.

Late Eighteenth Century
> Plates 21, 22, 23, 24, 25, 26, 27, 28, 29, 30, 31, 32, 37, 38,
> 39, 40, 41, 42, 43, 44, 68, 73, 74, 75, 76, 77, 78, 79,
> 80, 81, 82, 83, 91, 92, 93, 94, 95, 96, 97, 104, 105,
> 106.

Early Nineteenth Century
> Plates 33, 45, 46, 47, 48, 49, 50, 51, 52, 53, 54, 55, 56, 83,
> 84, 85, 86, 98, 99, 100, 101, 102, 103.

Plate I

COLONIAL INTERIORS

JOHN WARD HOUSE
SALEM, MASS.

(Mid-Seventeenth Century)

(Mid-Seventeenth Century) STEPHEN SWETT HOUSE *(See Plate 110)*
NEWBURY, MASS.

(See Plate 110)

(Mid-Seventeenth Century)

STEPHEN SWETT HOUSE
NEWBURY, MASS.

(Mid-Seventeenth Century)

JOHN WARD HOUSE
SALEM, MASS.

(Late Seventeenth Century)   CAPEN HOUSE
                                            TOPSFIELD, MASS.

(Late Seventeenth Century)   JOHN WHIPPLE HOUSE
                                            IPSWICH, MASS.

(Late Seventeenth Century)

JOHN WHIPPLE HOUSE
IPSWICH, MASS.

Plate 6

COLONIAL INTERIORS

(*Late Seventeenth Century*)

CAPTAIN LEE HOUSE
EAST LYME, CONN.

Plate 7

COLONIAL INTERIORS

(Late Seventeenth Century)

Capen House
Topsfield, Mass.

(Late Seventeenth Century)

HART-BURNHAM HOUSE
IPSWICH, MASS.

(Early Eighteenth Century)

STENTON
GERMANTOWN, PA.

(Early Eighteenth Century)   HENRY SEWALL HOUSE
SECRETARY, MD.

Plate 10

COLONIAL INTERIORS

(Early Eighteenth Century)

HENRY SEWALL HOUSE
SECRETARY, MD.

Plate 11

COLONIAL INTERIORS

(*Early Eighteenth Century*)

LOWER BRANDON
PRINCE GEORGE COUNTY, VA.

(Early Eighteenth Century)   ADDEN HOUSE
                                               READING, MASS.

(Early Eighteenth Century)   MORRIS HOUSE
                                               NEW HAVEN, CONN.

(Mid-Eighteenth Century)

Isaac Royall House
Medford, Mass.

(Mid-Eighteenth Century)

Governor Wentworth House
Portsmouth, N. H.

(Mid-Eighteenth Century)   CHAMPION HOUSE
EAST HADDAM, CONN.

(Mid-Eighteenth Century)   WHITBY HALL
WEST PHILADELPHIA, PA.

Plate 15

COLONIAL INTERIORS

GLEBE HOUSE
WOODBURY, CONN.

(*Mid-Eighteenth Century*)

COLONIAL INTERIORS

Plate 16

(*Mid-Eighteenth Century*)

ISAAC ROYALL HOUSE
MEDFORD, MASS.

COLONEL WILLOUGHBY TEBBS HOUSE
DUMFRIES, VA.

(See Plate 122)

Plate 18

(Mid-Eighteenth Century)   COLONEL WILLOUGHBY TEBBS HOUSE   *(See Plate* 122*)*
DUMFRIES, VA.

Plate 19

COLONIAL INTERIORS

(Mid-Eighteenth Century)

WAYSIDE INN
SOUTH SUDBURY, MASS.

Plate 20

COLONIAL INTERIORS

(Mid-Eighteenth Century)

WHITBY HALL
WEST PHILADELPHIA, PA.

(Mid-Eighteenth Century)

THE OLD MANSE
CONCORD, MASS.

(Late Eighteenth Century)

KITTRIDGE HOUSE
NORTH ANDOVER, MASS.

(Late Eighteenth Century)   QUINCY HOUSE
                                               QUINCY, MASS.

(Late Eighteenth Century)   McCreery House   *(See Plate* 108)
                    JOHNSON'S HOLLOW, LITCHFIELD COUNTY, CONN.

Plate 23

COLONIAL INTERIORS

(*Late Eighteenth Century*)

McCreery House

Johnson's Hollow, Litchfield County, Conn.

(*See Plate* 108)

(Late Eighteenth Century)   McCreery House   *(See Plate* 107)
Johnson's Hollow, Litchfield County, Conn.

(Late Eighteenth Century)   Jeremiah Lee House
Marblehead, Mass.

Plate 25

COLONIAL INTERIORS

(Late Eighteenth Century)

JEREMIAH LEE HOUSE
MARBLEHEAD, MASS.

Plate 26

COLONIAL INTERIORS

(Late Eighteenth Century)

JEREMIAH LEE HOUSE
MARBLEHEAD, MASS.

(Late Eighteenth Century)   MAJOR NICHOLAS DAVIS HOUSE   *(See Plate* 109)
                                          LIMINGTON, MAINE

(Late Eighteenth Century)   JEREMIAH LEE HOUSE
                                          MARBLEHEAD, MASS.

(See Plate 117)

(Late Eighteenth Century)   *(See Plate 116)*

WEBB HOUSE
WETHERSFIELD, CONN.

Plate 29

COLONIAL INTERIORS

(See Plate 118)

(Late Eighteenth Century)

WEBB HOUSE
WETHERSFIELD, CONN.

Plate 30

COLONIAL INTERIORS

(Late Eighteenth Century)

DAUNTLESS CLUB
ESSEX, CONN.

Plate 31

COLONIAL INTERIORS

(Late Eighteenth Century)

TOOKERMANN HOUSE
DOVER, DEL.

Plate 32

COLONIAL INTERIORS

(Late Eighteenth Century)

THE ADMIRAL COWLES HOUSE
OLDGATE, FARMINGTON, CONN.

(See Plate 119)

(Early Nineteenth Century)

PIERCE-NICHOLS HOUSE
SALEM, MASS.

Plate 35

(Mid-Eighteenth Century)

GOVERNOR WENTWORTH HOUSE
PORTSMOUTH, N. H.

(Mid-Eighteenth Century)

SHIRLEY
CHARLES CITY COUNTY, VA.

Plate 37

COLONIAL INTERIORS

(Mid-Eighteenth Century)

DALTON CLUB
NEWBURYPORT, MASS.

(Late Eighteenth Century)

JEREMIAH LEE HOUSE
MARBLEHEAD, MASS.

(Mid-Eighteenth Century)   *(See Plate* 120*)*

DALTON CLUB
NEWBURYPORT, MASS.

(Late Eighteenth Century)

MOUNT PLEASANT
FAIRMOUNT PARK, PHILADELPHIA, PA.

Plate 39

COLONIAL INTERIORS

(Late Eighteenth Century)

80 Federal Street
Salem, Mass.

(Mid-Eighteenth Century)

Champion House
East Haddam, Conn.

(Late Eighteenth Century)

48 BRIDGE STREET
SALEM, MASS.

(Late Eighteenth Century)

10 CHESTNUT STREET
NORTH ANDOVER, MASS.

(Late Eighteenth Century)

SAMUEL MATHER HOUSE
OLD LYME, CONN.

(Late Eighteenth Century)

JEREMIAH LEE HOUSE
MARBLEHEAD, MASS.

Plate 42

COLONIAL INTERIORS

(Late Eighteenth Century)

COOK-OLIVER HOUSE
SALEM, MASS.

Plate 43

(Late Eighteenth Century)

402 SOUTH FRONT STREET
PHILADELPHIA, PA.

(Late Eighteenth Century)

THIRD AND DELANCEY STREETS
PHILADELPHIA, PA.

(Late Eighteenth Century)

JESSUP HOUSE
WESTPORT, CONN.

(Late Eighteenth Century)

UPSALA
GERMANTOWN, PA.

(Late Eighteenth Century)

80 FEDERAL STREET
SALEM, MASS.

(Early Nineteenth Century)

14 PICKMAN STREET
SALEM, MASS.

(Early Nineteenth Century)   THE OCTAGON HOUSE
                                               WASHINGTON, D. C.

(Early Nineteenth Century)   ELM STREET
                                               SALEM, MASS.

Plate 47

COLONIAL INTERIORS

THE OCTAGON HOUSE
WASHINGTON, D. C.

(Early Nineteenth Century)

(Early Nineteenth Century)   OAK HILL
PEABODY, MASS.

(Early Nineteenth Century)   393 ESSEX STREET
SALEM, MASS.

(Early Nineteenth Century)

WISTER HOUSE
GERMANTOWN, PA.

(Early Nineteenth Century)   PIERCE-NICHOLS HOUSE
                                                         SALEM, MASS.

PIERCE-NICHOLS HOUSE
SALEM, MASS.

(Early Nineteenth Century)   ESSEX INSTITUTE
                                      SALEM, MASS.

(Early Nineteenth Century)   RICHARD DERBY HOUSE
                                       SALEM, MASS.

Plate 53

COLONIAL INTERIORS

OAK HILL
PEABODY, MASS.

(*Early Nineteenth Century*)

Plate 54

COLONIAL INTERIORS

(Early Nineteenth Century)
WATERS HOUSE
NEWBURYPORT, MASS.

(Early Nineteenth Century)
ATKINSON HOUSE
NEWBURYPORT, MASS.

(Early Nineteenth Century)
WATERS HOUSE
NEWBURYPORT, MASS.

SHORT HOUSE, SALEM, MASS.
202 ESSEX STREET, SALEM, MASS. (INSERT)

(Early Nineteenth Century)

SHORT HOUSE, SALEM, MASS.
CHESTNUT STREET, SALEM, MASS. (INSERT)

(Early Nineteenth Century)

(Early Nineteenth Century)   LINDALL ANDREWS HOUSE
                                      SALEM, MASS.

(Early Nineteenth Century)   393 ESSEX STREET
                                      SALEM, MASS.

Plate 57

COLONIAL INTERIORS

WINSLOW HOUSE
MARSHFIELD, MASS.

(Mid-Seventeenth Century)

Plate 58

COLONIAL INTERIORS

(Mid-Seventeenth Century)   HANCOCK-CLARKE HOUSE
LEXINGTON, MASS.

(Mid-Eighteenth Century)   168 DERBY STREET
SALEM, MASS.

Plate 59

(Late Seventeenth Century)

CRADDOCK HOUSE
MEDFORD, MASS.

Plate 60

COLONIAL INTERIORS

(Early Eighteenth Century)

MORRIS HOUSE
NEW HAVEN, CONN.

(Mid-Eighteenth Century)

GEORGE CABOT HOUSE
BEVERLY, MASS.

Plate 61

(Early Eighteenth Century)

HENRY SEWALL HOUSE
SECRETARY, MD.

Plate 62

COLONIAL INTERIORS

(*Early Eighteenth Century*)

WESTOVER
CHARLES CITY COUNTY, VA.

Plate 63

COLONIAL INTERIORS

(*Early Eighteenth Century*)

LOWER BRANDON
PRINCE GEORGE COUNTY, VA.

Plate 64

COLONIAL INTERIORS

(Mid-Eighteenth Century)   WHITBY HALL
WEST PHILADELPHIA, PA.

(Early Eighteenth Century)   GLEBE HOUSE
WOODBURY, CONN.

Plate 65

COLONIAL INTERIORS

(Mid-Eighteenth Century)

WHITBY HALL,
WEST PHILADELPHIA, PA.

(Early Eighteenth Century)

ROXBOROUGH
PHILADELPHIA, PA.

(Mid-Eighteenth Century)
TUCKAHOE
GOOCHLAND COUNTY, VA.

(Mid-Eighteenth Century)
INDEPENDENCE HALL
PHILADELPHIA, PA.

Plate 67

COLONIAL INTERIORS

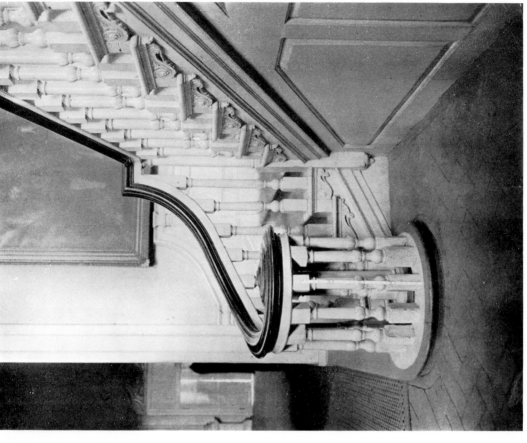

(Mid-Eighteenth Century)

INDEPENDENCE HALL
PHILADELPHIA, PA.

(Mid-Eighteenth Century) GOVERNOR WENTWORTH HOUSE
PORTSMOUTH, N. H.

Plate 68

COLONIAL INTERIORS

(Mid-Eighteenth Century)

WHITEY HALL,
WEST PHILADELPHIA, PA.

(Late Eighteenth Century)

SOUTH SIXTH STREET
PHILADELPHIA, PA.

(Mid-Eighteenth Century)

WHITBY HALL
WEST PHILADELPHIA, PA.

Plate 70

COLONIAL INTERIORS

(Mid-Eighteenth Century)

CLIVEDEN
GERMANTOWN, PA.

Plate 71

COLONIAL INTERIORS

(Mid-Eighteenth Century)

HOPE LODGE
WHITEMARSH, PA.

(Mid-Eighteenth Century)

9 ELM STREET
SALEM, MASS.

Plate 72

COLONIAL INTERIORS

(Mid-Seventeenth Century)   REBECCA NURSE HOUSE
DANVERS, MASS.

(Late Seventeenth Century)   CAPEN HOUSE
TOPSFIELD, MASS.

(Late Eighteenth Century)

JEREMIAH LEE HOUSE
MARBLEHEAD, MASS.

Plate 74

COLONIAL INTERIORS

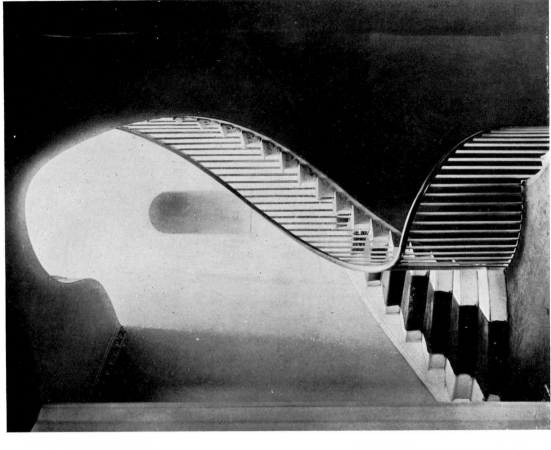

(Late Eighteenth Century) 40 BEACON STREET
BOSTON, MASS.

(Late Eighteenth Century) WHITEHALL
ANNE ARUNDEL COUNTY, MD.

Plate 75

(Late Eighteenth Century)

KITTRIDGE HOUSE
NORTH ANDOVER, MASS.

Plate 76

COLONIAL INTERIORS

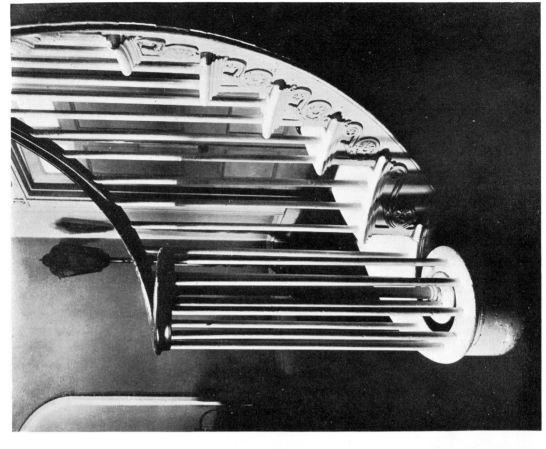

(Late Eighteenth Century)   40 BEACON STREET
                                 BOSTON, MASS.

(Late Eighteenth Century)   80 FEDERAL STREET
                                 SALEM, MASS.

(*Late Eighteenth Century*)

SIGOURNEY HOUSE
HARTFORD, CONN.

(Late Eighteenth Century)

BOWKER HOUSE
SALEM, MASS.

(Late Eighteenth Century)

FRONT STREET
PHILADELPHIA, PA.

Plate 80

COLONIAL INTERIORS

(Late Eighteenth Century)

9 ELM STREET
SALEM, MASS.

(Late Eighteenth Century)

168 DERBY STREET
SALEM, MASS.

Plate 81

COLONIAL INTERIORS

(*Late Eighteenth Century*)

KITTRIDGE HOUSE
NORTH ANDOVER, MASS.

Plate 82

(Late Eighteenth Century)

ROCHAMBEAU-VERNON HOUSE
NEWPORT, R. I.

Plate 83

COLONIAL INTERIORS

(Early Nineteenth Century)

WATERS HOUSE
SALEM, MASS.

(Late Eighteenth Century)

COOK-OLIVER HOUSE
SALEM, MASS.

Plate 84

COLONIAL INTERIORS

(Early Nineteenth Century)   HIGH STREET
DANVERSPORT, MASS.

(Early Nineteenth Century)   210 ESSEX STREET
SALEM, MASS.

202½ ESSEX STREET
SALEM, MASS.

Plate 86

COLONIAL INTERIORS

(Early Nineteenth Century) MOSES WILLIAMS HOUSE
JAMAICA PLAINS, MASS.

(Early Nineteenth Century) THEODORE BAGLEY HOUSE
BRISTOL, R. I.

Plate 87

COLONIAL INTERIORS

(Mid-Eighteenth Century)   DALTON CLUB
NEWBURYPORT, MASS.

ISAAC ROYALL HOUSE
MEDFORD, MASS.   *(Mid-Eighteenth Century)*

Plate 88

COLONIAL INTERIORS

Hope Lodge
Whitemarsh, Pa.

(Mid-Eighteenth Century)

Plate 89

COLONIAL INTERIORS

(*Mid-Eighteenth Century*)

HARWOOD HOUSE
ANNAPOLIS, MD.

(*Mid-Eighteenth Century*)

SHIRLEY
CHARLES CITY COUNTY, VA.

Plate 90

COLONIAL INTERIORS

(Mid-Eighteenth Century)   CHAMPION HOUSE
EAST HADDAM, CONN.

(Mid-Eighteenth Century)   SALTONSTALL HOUSE
HAVERHILL, MASS.

Plate 91

COLONIAL INTERIORS

(*Late Eighteenth Century*)   MOUNT PLEASANT
PHILADELPHIA, PA.

(*Mid-Eighteenth Century*)   BELMONT
FAIRMOUNT PARK, PHILADELPHIA, PA.

(*Mid-Eighteenth Century*)   HOPE LODGE
WHITEMARSH, PA.

Plate 92

COLONIAL INTERIORS

(Late Eighteenth Century)

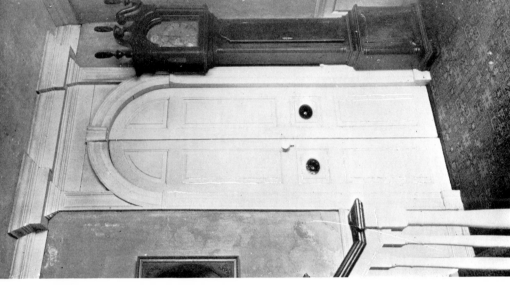

(Mid-Eighteenth Century)
TOOKERMANN HOUSE
DOVER, DEL.

SEWALL HOUSE
YORK, MAINE

COOK-OLIVER HOUSE
SALEM, MASS.

(Late Eighteenth Century)

Plate 93

COLONIAL INTERIORS

(Late Eighteenth Century)

MOUNT PLEASANT
PHILADELPHIA, PA.

(Late Eighteenth Century)

ROCKINGHAM HOTEL
PORTSMOUTH, N. H.

Plate 94

COLONIAL INTERIORS

(*Late Eighteenth Century*)   HUNTINGTON HOUSE
OLD LYME, CONN.

(*Late Eighteenth Century*)   THE ADMIRAL COWLES HOUSE
OLDGATE, FARMINGTON, CONN.

(*Late Eighteenth Century*)

GEORGE READ HOUSE
NEW CASTLE, DEL.

(Late Eighteenth Century)   GEORGE READ HOUSE
                                                NEW CASTLE, DEL.

Plate 97

COLONIAL INTERIORS

(*Late Eighteenth Century*)
COOK-OLIVER HOUSE
SALEM, MASS.

(*Late Eighteenth Century*)
STEWART HOUSE
JAMAICA PLAINS, MASS.

(*Late Eighteenth Century*)
SEWALL HOUSE
YORK, MAINE

Plate 98

COLONIAL INTERIORS

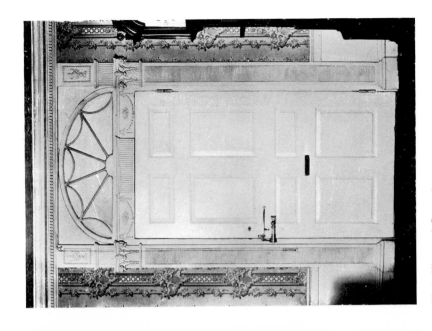

(Early Nineteenth Century)
PIERCE-NICHOLS HOUSE
SALEM, MASS.

(Early Nineteenth Century)
PIERCE-NICHOLS HOUSE
SALEM, MASS.

(Early Nineteenth Century)
ESSEX STREET
SALEM, MASS.

Plate 99

COLONIAL INTERIORS

OAK HILL.
PEABODY, MASS.

(Early Nineteenth Century)

Plate 100

COLONIAL INTERIORS

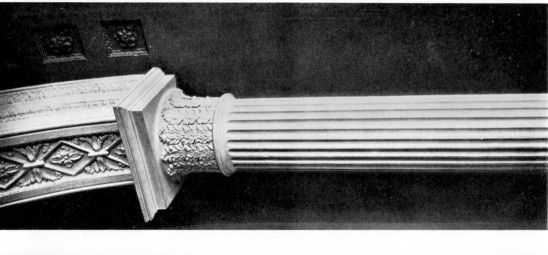

THE OCTAGON HOUSE
WASHINGTON, D. C.

(Early Nineteenth Century)

Plate 101

COLONIAL INTERIORS

(Early Nineteenth Century)   SAMUEL FOWLER HOUSE
DANVERSPORT, MASS.

(Early Nineteenth Century)   THE OCTAGON HOUSE
WASHINGTON, D. C.

Plate 102

COLONIAL INTERIORS

(Early Nineteenth Century)   PIERCE-NICHOLS HOUSE
SALEM, MASS.

(Early Nineteenth Century)   PIERCE-NICHOLS HOUSE
SALEM, MASS.

(Early Nineteenth Century)   OAK HILL
PEABODY, MASS.

Plate 103

COLONIAL INTERIORS

(Mid-Eighteenth Century)

DALTON CLUB
NEWBURYPORT, MASS.

(Early Nineteenth Century)

PIERCE-NICHOLS HOUSE
SALEM, MASS.

Plate 104

COLONIAL INTERIORS

(Late Eighteenth Century)   Kittridge House
North Andover, Mass.

(Mid-Eighteenth Century)   Isaac Royall House
Medford, Mass.

Plate 105

COLONIAL INTERIORS

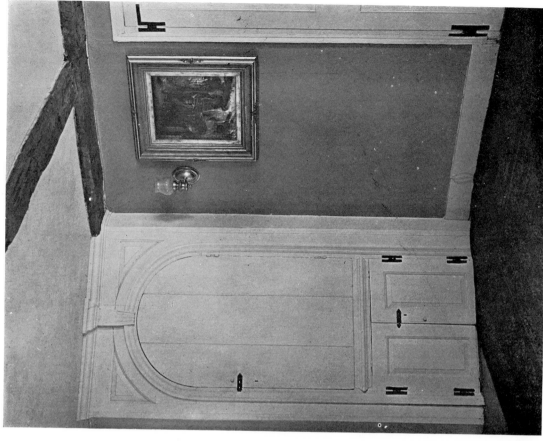

(Early Eighteenth Century)

MORRIS HOUSE
NEW HAVEN, CONN.

(Late Eighteenth Century)

WEBB HOUSE
WETHERSFIELD, CONN.

Plate 106

COLONIAL INTERIORS

(Late Eighteenth Century)   48 BRIDGE STREET
SALEM, MASS.

(Late Eighteenth Century)   JEREMIAH LEE HOUSE
MARBLEHEAD, MASS.

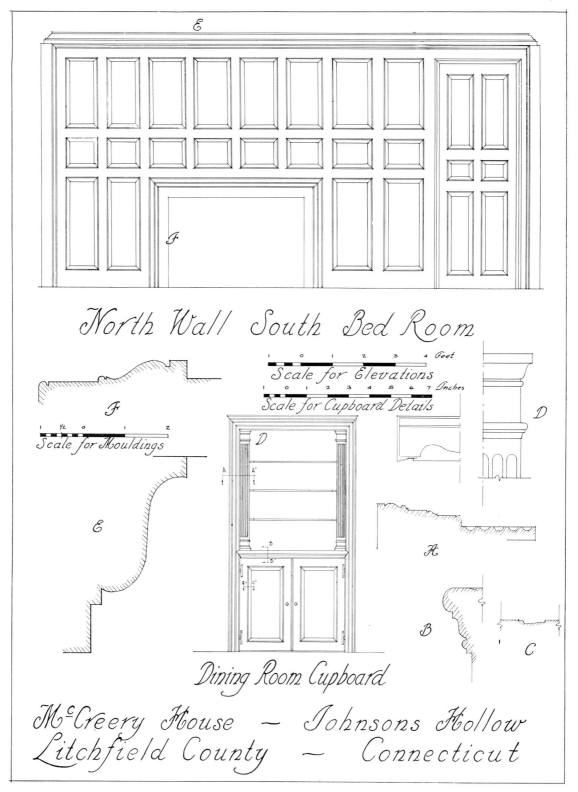

North Wall South Bed Room

Scale for Elevations

Scale for Cupboard Details

Scale for Mouldings

Dining Room Cupboard

McCreery House — Johnsons Hollow
Litchfield County — Connecticut

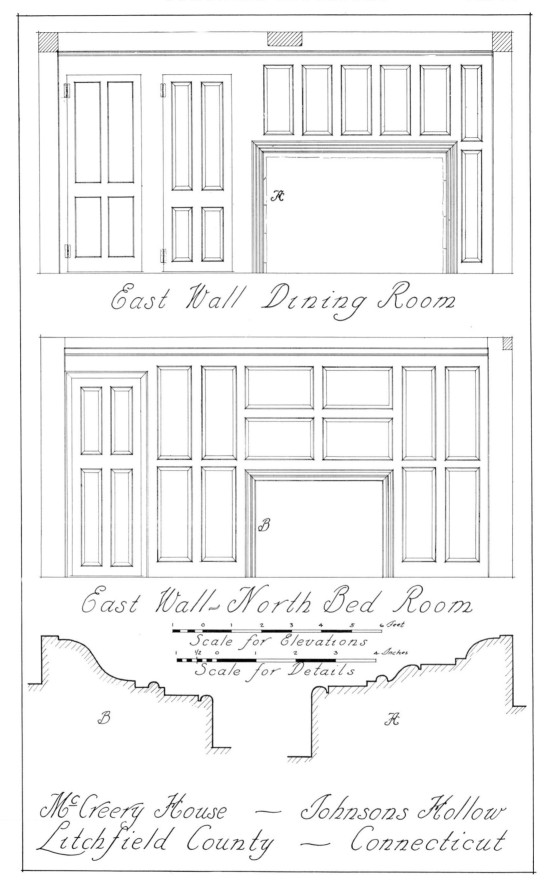

East Wall Dining Room

East Wall~North Bed Room

1 0 1 2 3 4 5 6 *feet*
Scale for Elevations
1½ 0 1 2 3 4 *Inches*
Scale for Details

Mc Creery House — Johnsons Hollow
Litchfield County — Connecticut

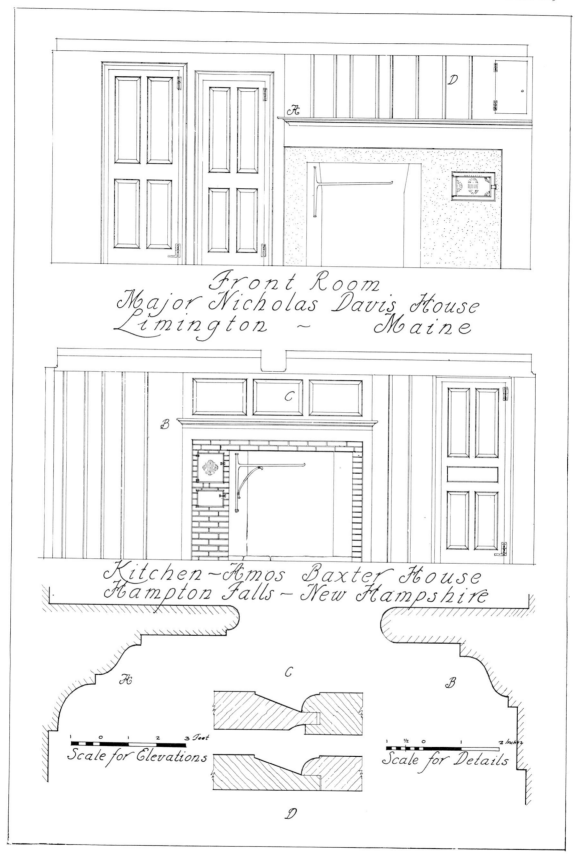

Front Room
Major Nicholas Davis House
Limington ~   Maine

Kitchen ~ Amos Baxter House
Hampton Falls ~ New Hampshire

Scale for Elevations

Scale for Details

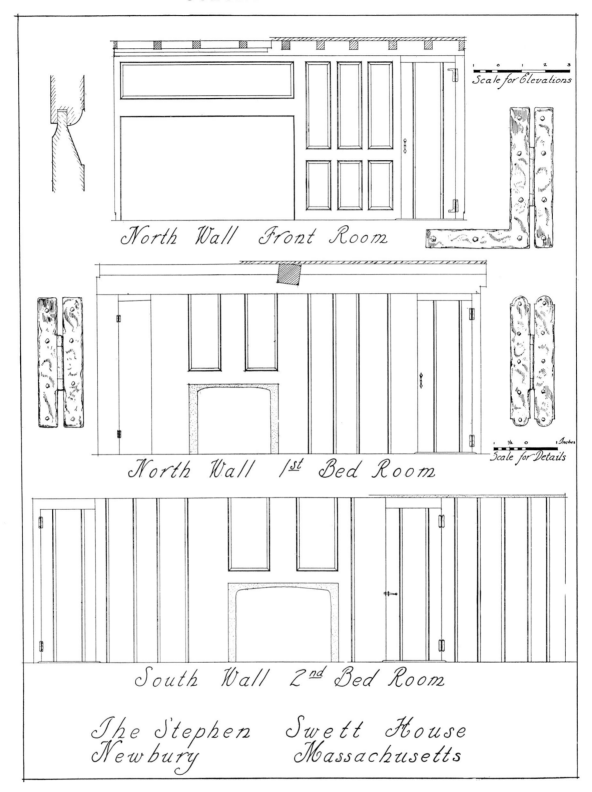

North Wall Front Room

Scale for Elevations

North Wall 1ˢᵗ Bed Room

Scale for Details

South Wall 2ⁿᵈ Bed Room

*The Stephen Swett House
Newbury Massachusetts*

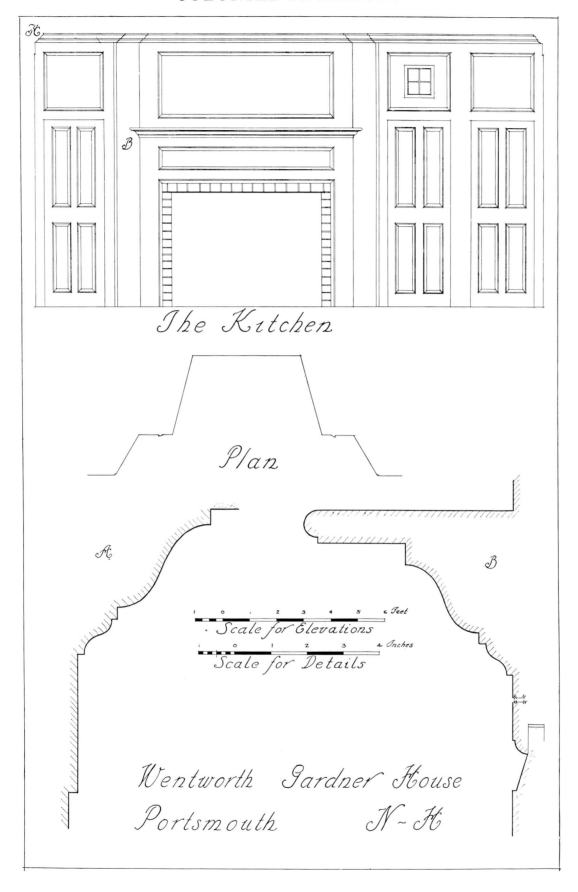

The Kitchen

Plan

Scale for Elevations

Scale for Details

Wentworth Gardner House

Portsmouth   N ~ H

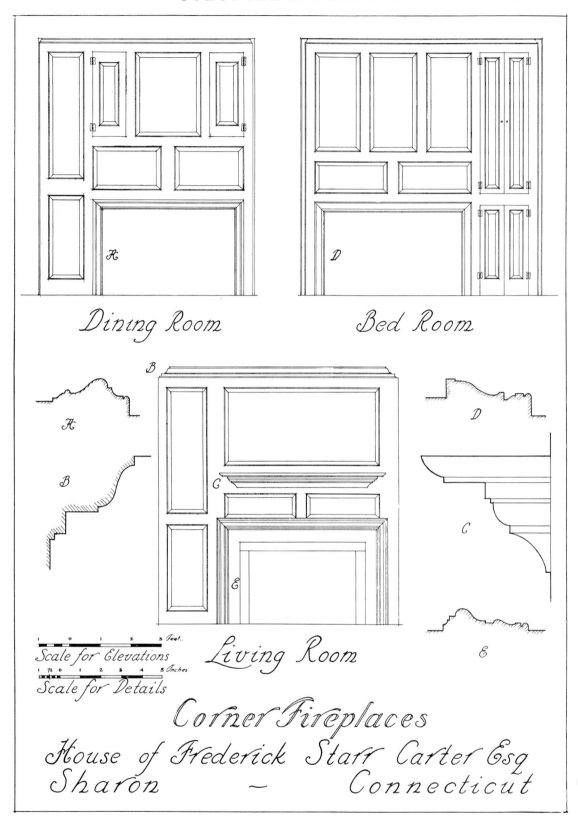

Dining Room   Bed Room

Scale for Elevations

Scale for Details

Living Room

Corner Fireplaces
House of Frederick Starr Carter Esq
Sharon   —   Connecticut

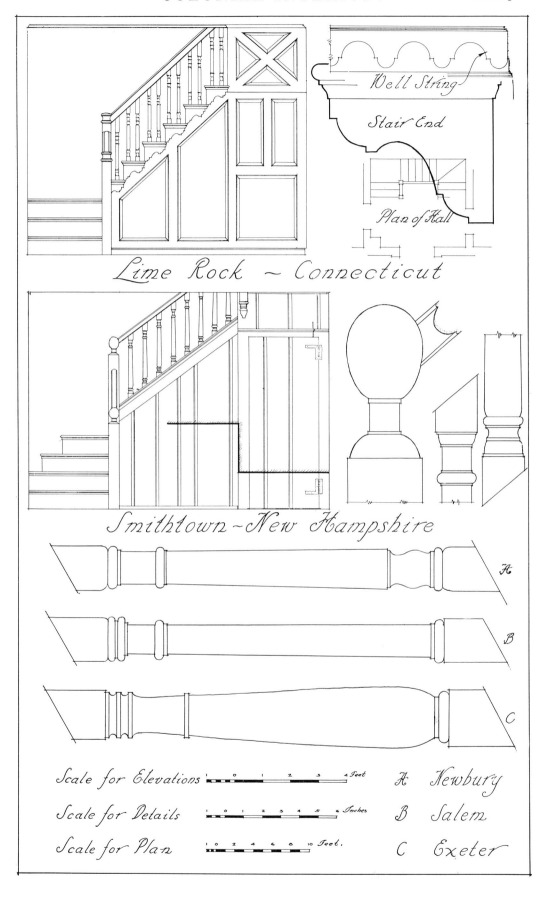

Well String

Stair End

Plan of Hall

Lime Rock ~ Connecticut

Smithtown ~ New Hampshire

A

B

C

Scale for Elevations   Feet   A   Newbury

Scale for Details   Inches   B   Salem

Scale for Plan   Feet   C   Exeter

Elevation

Scale for Elevation

Scale for Details

Fireplace Side of South Parlor
Wentworth – Gardner House
Portsmouth – New Hampshire

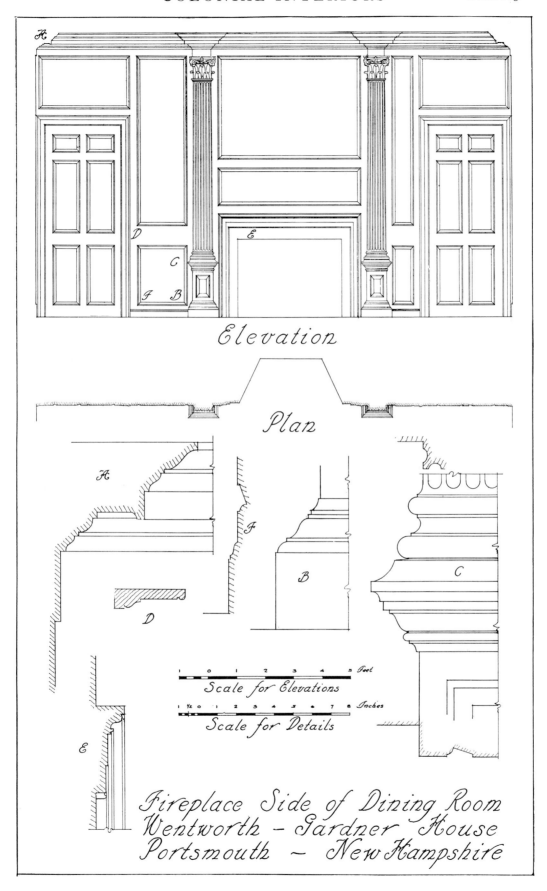

Elevation

Plan

Scale for Elevations

Scale for Details

Fireplace Side of Dining Room
Wentworth — Gardner House
Portsmouth — New Hampshire

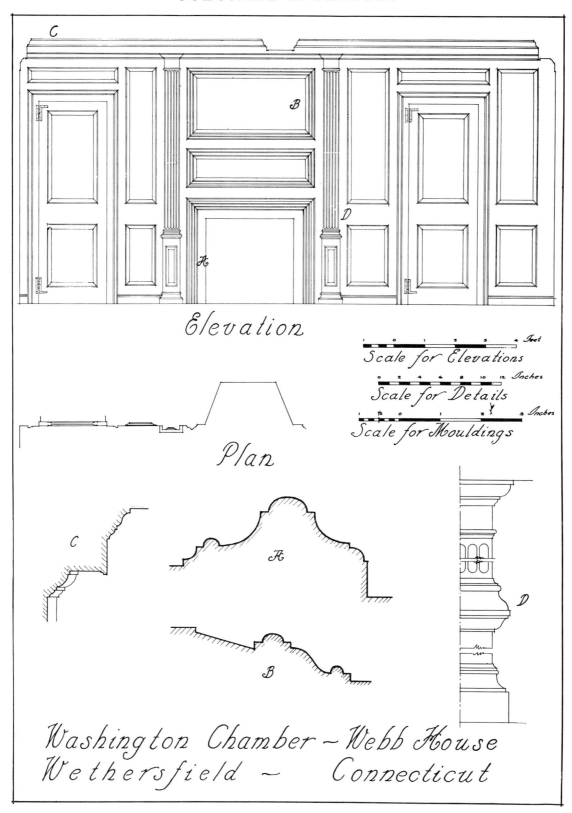

Elevation

Scale for *Elevations*

Scale for *Details*

Scale for *Mouldings*

Plan

Washington Chamber — Webb House
Wethersfield —   Connecticut

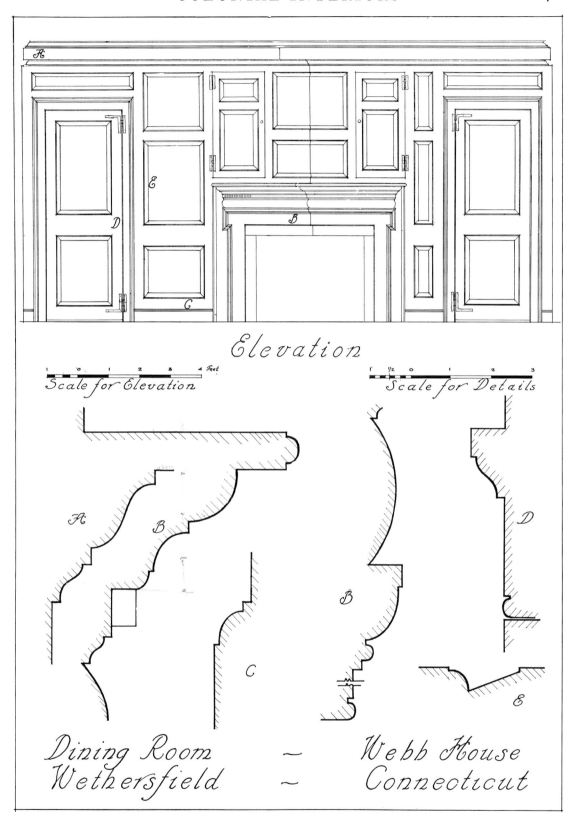

Elevation

Scale for Elevation   Scale for Details

Dining Room   ~   Webb House
Wethersfield   ~   Connecticut

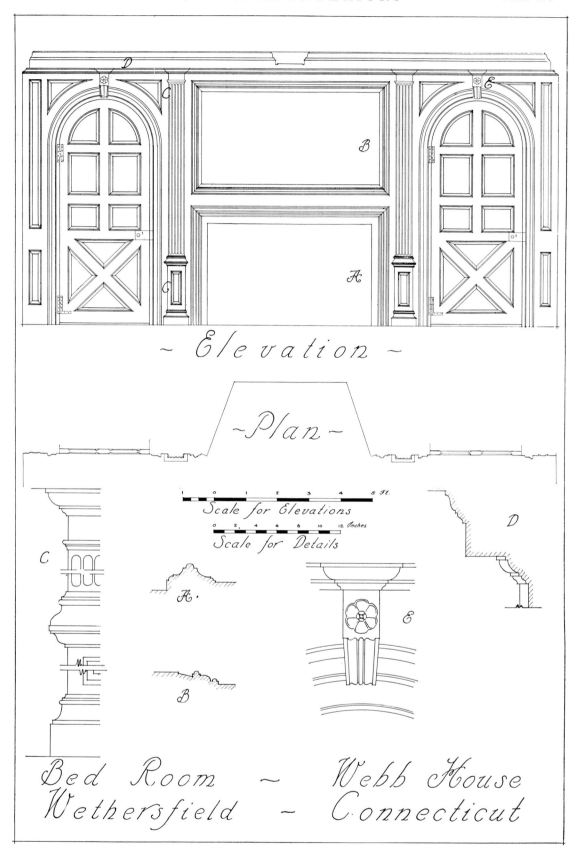

~ *Elevation* ~

~ *Plan* ~

Scale for Elevations

Scale for Details

Bed Room   ~   Webb House
Wethersfield   ~   Connecticut

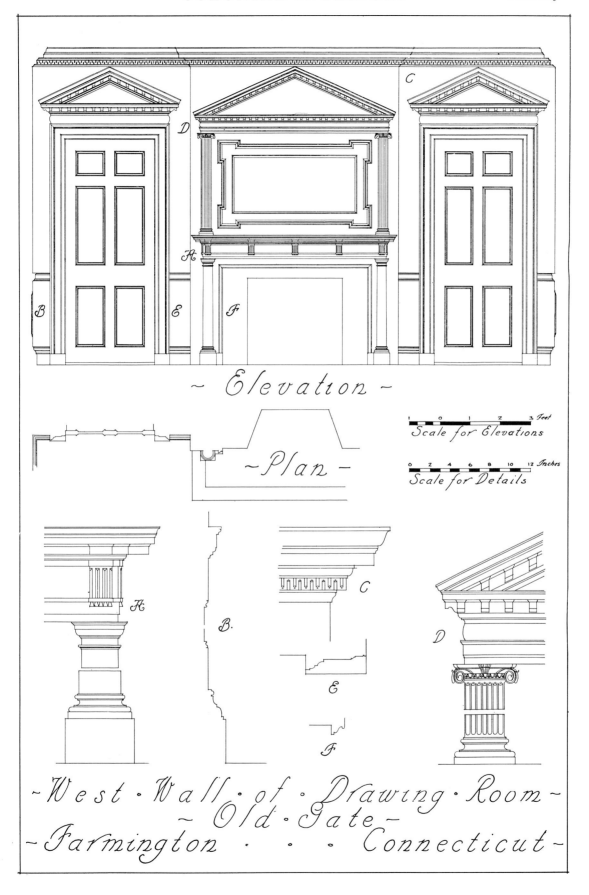

~ Elevation ~

~ Plan ~

Scale for Elevations

Scale for Details

~ West · Wall · of · Drawing · Room ~
~ Old · Gate ~
~ Farmington · · · Connecticut ~

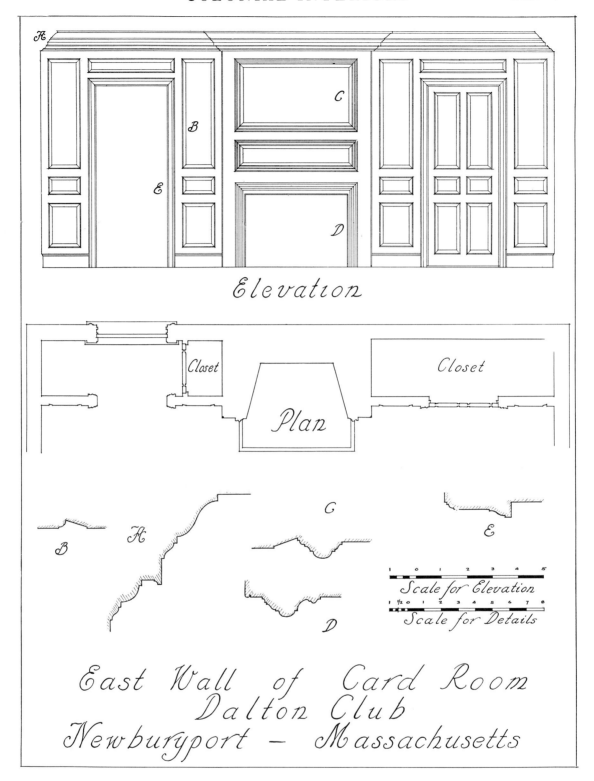

Elevation

Closet *Closet*

Plan

Scale for Elevation

Scale for Details

East Wall of Card Room
Dalton Club
Newburyport — Massachusetts

Elevation of East Wall Front Room

China Closet

Plan

Scale for Elevations

Scale for Details

Herman B. Smith House
Lime Rock ~ Connecticut

Plan

E

1762

Before Restoration

~ The · North · Wall ~

B

A

A

Flat Soffit

B

E

C

D

C

D

The South Wall

Colonel Willoughby Tebbs House
Dumfries ~ Prince William County
Virginia

Scale for Elevation

Scale for Details

Scale for Plan

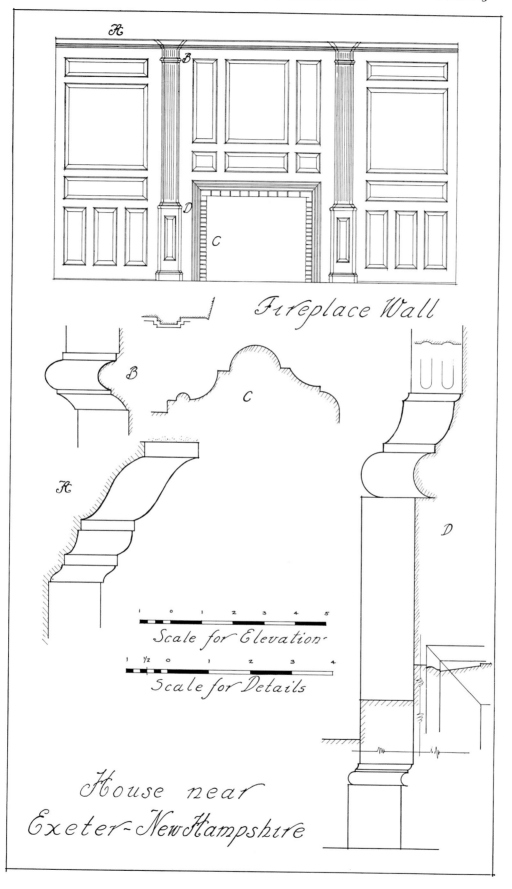

Fireplace Wall

Scale for Elevation

Scale for Details

House near
Exeter-New Hampshire

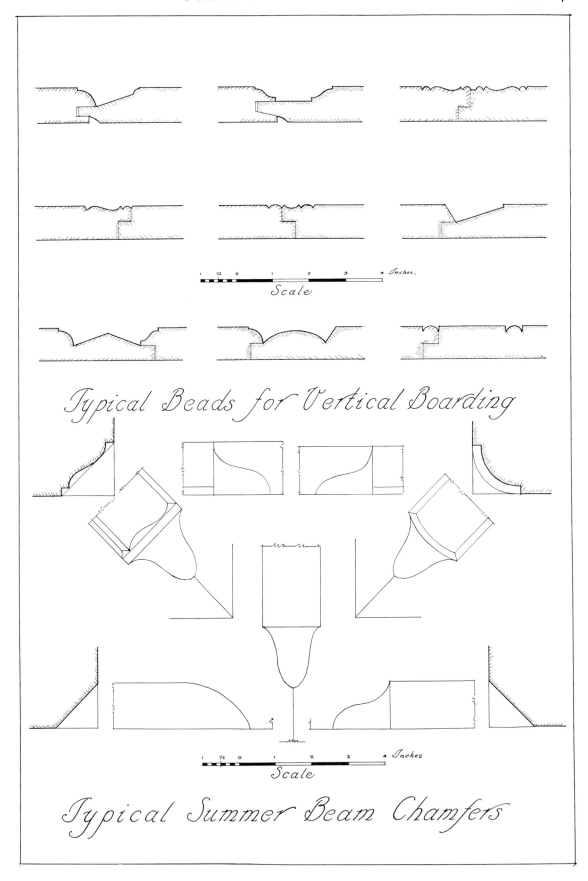

Typical Beads for Vertical Boarding

Scale

Typical Summer Beam Chamfers

Scale

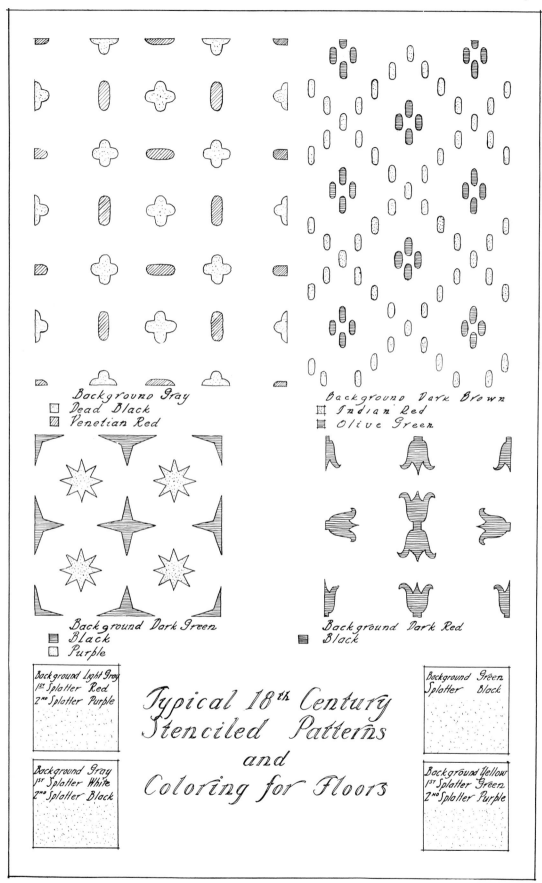

Background Gray
☐ Dead Black
▨ Venetian Red

Background Dark Brown
⊟ Indian Red
▦ Olive Green

Background Dark Green
▥ Black
☐ Purple

Background Dark Red
▦ Black

Background Light Gray
1ˢᵗ Splatter Red
2ⁿᵈ Splatter Purple

Background Gray
1ˢᵗ Splatter White
2ⁿᵈ Splatter Black

Background Green
Splatter Black

Background Yellow
1ˢᵗ Splatter Green
2ⁿᵈ Splatter Purple

*Typical 18th Century
Stenciled Patterns
and
Coloring for Floors*